Gemstone & Crystal ELIXIRS

Potions for Love Health Wealth Energy and Success

Robert W. Wood D.Hp
(Diploma in Hypnotherapy)

Rosewood Publishing

First published in U.K. 2002
By Rosewood Publishing
P.O. Box 219, Huddersfield,
West Yorkshire HD2 2YT

www.rosewood-gifts.co.uk

Revised cover and
Re-printed in 2011

Copy-editing
Margaret Wakefield BA (Hons) London
www.euroreportage.co.uk

Cover photograph by
Andrew Caveney BA (Hons)
www.andrewcaveneyphotography.co.uk

Cover and layout re-designed by
AJ Typesetting
www.ajtype.co.uk

Printed in Great Britain by
Delta Design & Print Ltd
www.deltaleeds.co.uk

ISBN 978-0-9532930-3-2 BK4

Gemstones & Crystal Elixirs

Let your imagination fly you, on the wings of Love,
Into an ancient world of Magic, Mystery & Imagination.
By changing the way we think,
we can change the future.

o0o

"Elixir of Life":
An alchemical preparation
capable of prolonging life;
A liquid containing a medicine.

o0o

A Power Within

From the dawning of time, and hidden deep inside the subconscious mind within each and every one of us, there lies an amazing, invisible, gentle giant. One that can be stirred when touched by stories of Myths, Magic and Mysteries

Think of the popularity of the Harry Potter films, or Lord of the Rings. Who hasn't heard of King Arthur and the Round Table, or Merlin the magician? We like stories, especially mysteries; they feed our imaginations.

Now, in this book we're not describing a magic like that of magicians pulling rabbits out of hats.

We're talking of an ancient form of 'magic', the art of using lotions, potions, gemstones and crystals to awaken this giant within, to invoke the supernatural powers that we will need to help us change and influence future events.

Understand: we're not talking about witches riding on broomsticks or cooking up 'eye of newt' and 'toe of rat' in a bubbling cauldron. Instead, imagine a biochemist working in the very latest, air-conditioned, 'state-of-the-art' laboratory.

Today, science and technology are laying bare the secrets of the Universe; and one such secret that science has been investigating is the workings of the mind, both the conscious and the subconscious. However, our understanding of the power that's within the mind is still in its infancy. It seems that we are only now discovering just how amazing this 'power within' really is.

To discover this power that we are calling a gentle giant, let's try a little experiment. For example:- When you read the word 'witches and broomsticks', I'll almost guarantee you imagined an old woman in black. And when you read 'imagine a biochemist', you probably imagined him or her in a white coat. Most people do; we're programmed, and this effect that we call the 'imagination' was created by - well, if you believe in Darwin's theory you will say by evolution, or you may say by a universal life force that many today would call God. The fact is, we all possess this power, the power of imagination. We are the living proof.

Henry Ford couldn't have built motor cars before he had *'imagined'* he could.

A Dawning of an Age

If the Piscean age was the age of Jesus Christ the man, then could the Aquarian age be the age when the spiritual nature of the Christ can be fulfilled and realised in all of us. Perhaps this is what is meant by the term 'the second coming'.

Moving from a great age of Christian religion, as well as religions from Asia and the Orient, the coming age is one of humanity; one that is not separated by religions, beliefs, creeds or dogmas. Emerging is a Golden Age, characterised by people living as individuals with their own beliefs about the world - but living in harmony, without any personal judgement of others.

A Freedom to Choose

One of the greatest questions must be, can we change our fate? Can we indeed affect the future? Or does it all just depend on the spin of a coin? The answer, I believe, is: yes, we can, at least to the extent that we have free will - that is, we have a freedom to choose. How do we get help to change our future for the better? One way you are about to discover is with the help of Gemstone and Crystal Elixirs.

Do Elixirs Really Work?

I believe they do. To understand the 'how' and 'why', we need to look deeper into the three ingredients needed to produce a Gemstone and Crystal Elixir. Firstly there's water, and secondly, gemstone-crystals. But there's a third ingredient, often overlooked, but which I believe to be the most important ingredient of all: the Mind.

Firstly ... Water

Whoever is thirsty, let him come, and whoever wishes, let him take the free gift of the 'Water of Life'.

Rev 22.17-18

Imagine the flow of life being symbolised by water. It seeps into the areas of life that are inaccessible to other elements, which is one reason why it is associated with the subconscious, emotional and imaginative forces within the mind. Water is a unique substance, with amazing properties - either as a liquid, or a gas (in the form of steam), or even a solid (in the form of ice). Some describe it as a living substance, maybe with an energy of its own. It's even been suggested that water somehow has a memory, a structure that stores information, maybe in the same way genetic data is stored in the DNA.

Homeopathy

In homeopathy, for example, plant and animal extracts are dissolved into a solution. Most of the flower essences are prepared by floating the blooms in pure water for a number of hours. This is often called 'the sun method'. Others are prepared by boiling for an hour or so, this being more effective for the harder types of flowers and woody plants.

Mother Tincture

The mixture is then strained, and the resulting solution is known as the 'mother tincture'. Added to this solution is full strength 30-40% proof brandy, to act as a preservative. The 'mother tincture' is then diluted again, and again, and again; in fact, by the time the remedy reaches its final stage, it is unlikely that any of the original substance remains in the solution, and yet it still seems to remain effective. However, the lack of evidence that there is anything there other than just pure liquid, may explain why some sceptics find it difficult to accept the efficacy of homeopathy. Supporters, on the other hand, believe that the science of physics is not yet developed enough to explain the phenomenon.

Secondly ... Gemstones and Crystals

It has taken over 4,000 years to prove scientifically what ancient wisdom teaches: that there is a force in nature so powerful, and yet to most of us quite invisible.

Now faith is being sure of what we hope for and certain of what we do not see. This is what the ancients were commended for.

By faith we understand that the Universe was formed by God's command, so that what is seen was not made out of what was visible.

Hebrews 11.1- 4

It has taken quantum physics to show that solid matter is actually 99.9% empty space yet filled with energy. Now that we know that all matter is energy, looking at it this way may make it easier to understand how man can interact with gemstones and crystals.

Vibrations

Consider a tuning fork. When it is struck, and placed, vibrating, near the strings of a guitar or harp, only the string tuned to the same note or frequency will pick up the vibration and resonate. The rest of the strings will not; they remain unaffected.

The key to understanding the teachings of ancient wisdom may lie in the connection between the vibrations sent out by the perfect inner structure of crystals, and the human mind.

Crystals, unlike nature, have not evolved. It's said that they are the building blocks of the universe. They haven't changed; they are exactly the same today as they were billions of years ago. Some even suggest they can be likened to the 'control experiment' used by scientists to verify the results of a parallel experiment. The variable which is being investigated in the parallel experiment remains constant in the 'control'.

Bound by myths, magic and mysteries, crystals seem to help bring to light the many different historical world views that have arisen down the ages concerning this immutable link between ourselves and nature. However, the spiritual connection between humans and inanimate objects such as crystals is not confined to New Age or pagan beliefs. In the Bible, stones and rocks were a symbol of human spirit and a representation of the higher self. Christ is referred to as a `living rock'.

Gemstones and Crystals in the Bible

Gemstones and crystals are part of Creation. They have been written about for thousands of years, with some of the earliest writings being in the Scriptures. There's a piece in the Old Testament (Genesis) where God describes to Aaron, 'the first High Priest', how to produce a Breastplate, placing on it twelve gemstones and crystals. These twelve stones would represent the twelve tribes of Israel. Symbolically, there are twelve stones in Astrology to represent the cycle of life, and these are called birthstones.

Curiously, there is another list of twelve stones in the New Testament, here representing 'a New Jerusalem'. Even stranger for me was the discovery that the first foundation for the New Jerusalem was Jasper. Strange, because in my research I had already selected the same stone for Aries, which in Astrology is the first sign. The sixth foundation of the the New Jerusalem was Carnelian, and I had selected this stone for Virgo, the sixth sign in Astrology; while the twelfth foundation was Amethyst, which I had selected for Pisces, being the twelfth star sign. To discover how I got my selection of stones, you'll have to read my book 'Discover Why Crystal Healing Works', where I have given a fuller explanation of all the research I did.

Think of energy being channelled through crystals. However, crystals are only one form of tool, or catalyst, that helps to direct this inexplicable source of power, a power often referred to as the 'Universal Life Force'.

Elixirs

Whilst researching elixirs I often found conflicting information that only seemed to lead to more confusion, rather than clarify. So in an attempt to penetrate these mysteries, and especially Crystal Elixirs, I will focus only on elixirs and see if we can make some sense of it all. At the same time I believe we will discover a practical use for our newly gained knowledge.

A gemstone-crystal elixir is water into which a gemstone-crystal has been placed and left until the 'memory' of its health-giving or luck-changing vibrations is all that remains.

Warning
Some gemstone-crystals are unsuitable for producing elixirs, particular those that are soluble. Some gemstones and crystals should not be used under any circumstances as they contain poisonous toxins. However, all the gemstones and crystals mentioned in this book are quite safe. Do remember, though, to wash and clean them first.

It should go without saying that your choice of gemstones or crystals will depend on the results you want to achieve.

Gemstones and crystals have always been linked with Love, Health, Wealth, Prosperity, Energy and Success. Born from alchemy, a forerunner to our modern day chemistry, elixirs, lotions and potions were in times past only practised by a select few: priests, sages, holy men and magicians. Among these select few was Hildegard of Bingen. She was just one of the many famous recorded purveyors associated with gemstone elixirs.

Hildegard of Bingen

She was one of the outstanding females of the 12th century and probably of the entire Middle Ages. She was a painter, composer, poet, scientist, playwright, prophet, preacher, abbess – and a healer. Born in 1098, she lived until 1179, an impressive 81 years. From the time she was a young girl, Hildegard had experienced visions. Some of her ideas about Gemstones can be traced back to the Roman naturalist Pliny and other earlier authors such as Aristotle (4th century B.C.). Many of her directions or recipes involved the preparation of elixirs or the wearing of a stone, especially on the bare skin; soaking the stones in water or wine and then drinking the liquid or pouring it over the troubled spot. Hildegard claimed that angels described to her the healing properties of at least 25 stones. She describes putting an agate (stone) in water when the moon was full and leaving it there for three days and nights, then on the fourth day removing it and using the water for cooking the food for one who was suffering from a certain malady.

Feeling the need to share her visions with the world, at the age of 43 she decided to record what her visions had shown her. Hildegard consulted her confessor, who consulted the Abbot, who consulted the Archbishop of Mainz. Eventually, even the Pope was consulted, and all apparently agreed that these were true visions and her knowledge had come from angels, or at least some sacred source, and was worth recording.

Many of the earliest scholars believed that gemstones and crystals did have strange, often mysterious like powers.

Gemstones - Science or Myth?

If you take two quartz crystals and rub them together in the dark, you will see them light up quite spectacularly. Five thousand years ago, that would have been 'spooky' or even weird, certainly it would have been mind-blowing to anyone who didn't know the cause. Another example: if you put a lodestone near iron filings, the filings move, and people used to think this was magic. The stone, they thought, must possess mystical powers, or could even be alive. However, today we know that this stone acts like a magnet, and the effect is quite natural.

Because of all the mysticism surrounding gemstones and crystals, it is not surprising to find that some scholars believed gemstones and crystals were alive. In Aristotle's writings we find descriptions of stones changing colour, especially when their owners were in danger from attack or poisons. Stones were even ground down to dust and then taken as we would today take aspirin for a headache.

I have spent many years researching and analysing as much information as possible, much of it spanning over many thousands of years. I have finally, from all of my research, produced my list of 15 basic (non-soluble) healing stones (pages 15-16), plus a range of Power Gems. These are combinations of stones relating directly to specific requirements; for example: Love Potion - Rose Quartz, Amethyst and Carnelian; for Good Luck - Green Aventurine, Obsidian Snowflake and Moonstone. See page 16 for many more.

In the next chapter we will explore the final ingredient that I believe is essential in producing elixirs, and that's the power within the mind. A power we call 'imagination'.

To use your mind effectively
You must start by believing in its power.

Imagination and the Mind

Although it's easy to see the importance of the first two ingredients - water and crystals - the third part, the mind, may well be the most important, and therefore could hold the key. The mind is often spoken of as unique and multi-faceted. That's an understatement. It's rather like saying the Universe is big: factually true, but it doesn't even start to scratch the surface.

The greatest philosophers of all time have pondered about the mind, the body, our emotions and feelings. The Scriptures say we are created and made in God's image. If that's true, then think about this:

There isn't, as yet (and I don't think there will ever be) a computer that could drive a car like a human being does. Think about it; how much information does a driver of a car take in during a normal journey? Doesn't that give you an idea of just how special we humans are?

Philosophy

Every existing being - from an atom to a galaxy - is rooted in the same universal, life-creating reality.

It reveals itself in the purposeful, ordered and meaningful processes of nature as well as in the deepest recesses of the mind and spirit.

My quest, and that of many others, is not to impose any dogma, but to point toward the source of unity that's beyond all our differences.

Many scholars have described life as being like a journey. The purpose may be to discover its meaning. What we seek outside, we may already own. Many others who have lived, loved and dreamed have left their legacies for the rest of us, in the form of their thoughts, writings, poetry and pictures, their beliefs and religions. They have all tried to explain the reason, the 'Mystery of Life'.

Power of the Mind

Let us accept that thoughts and emotions are all forms of mental energy, and that they play a very significant part in our well-being. It's believed we can influence the state of our physical body, either beneficially or otherwise, by the way we think.

Imagine this as an idea: Maybe it's the energy in thought that powers up crystals, just as electricity powers up a computer. Your own strength of will helps to direct, focus and amplify. Our natural state is one of moving towards balance, not away.

There is an important and potentially very happy marriage between the spiritual, the mystical and the scientific world views. So keep an open mind. There are many different methods of looking at the nature of 'reality'. This is only one of them.

Visualisation

You are now beginning to explore new dimensions of 'reality'. You don't need a spaceship, or to be spaced out, to take this journey. Just the will to find out more about yourself, and an open mind as you now take your own special journey into the future. The brain cannot tell the difference between what is real and what is realistically imagined. That is why visualising is so powerful. Feeling, hearing, tasting, touching and smelling an imaginary experience is, as far as your brain's concerned, just as good as the 'reality', if the image had been real.

Have fun with your elixirs and your explorations. There is nothing unnatural about wishing to glimpse into the future or, for that matter, wishing to change it, particularly if you are given an opportunity to change it for the better.

Alchemy

Step back in time. Imagine yourself walking down one of the old Victorian shopping streets like the ones in York or Chester, and then coming across a shop with a sign outside saying 'Alchemy'. You go inside - and, surprisingly, it's more like a modern day café.

You pick up the menu, and as you read it, you quickly realise it isn't food they're selling but magic potions and lotions, all guaranteed to work. Who wouldn't be tempted to try them?

You read titles such as `to Remove Aches and Pains', 'Energy Booster', 'to Lift Depression', and the speciality of the house, 'The Elixir of Life'.

Then you notice ...

The chef's special:
A Love Potion

Highly recommended: ***Harmony***
For the more adventurous: ***An Aphrodisiac***

Try them if you dare!

On page 16 is a list of the different elixirs and their formulas. So choose the one best suited to your desires.

Decide on the desired effect - are you seeking Love, Luck, Prosperity, Harmony, or something else? Next, choose the gemstone or crystal that in your opinion is best suited to your needs. You can use one, two or three of them, and you will find help on pages 15-16.

The Basics – Preparation

Start by purchasing two mineral water bottles, half-litre size with large screw tops. Empty one of the bottles and then place a label onto it, naming the elixir. For example it might be a Love Potion or maybe a Healer or even an Energy Booster. The choice is yours.

You may find the label puzzling, but it's really very important. Why? Because it acts on the mind, as an affirmation, and the mind works well with affirmations. There is a part of the brain that responds well to subliminal persuasion, so every time you use your elixirs, the act of reading the label reinforces within the mind your objectives, your desires. It reminds your brain what it is that you are asking for. So – make sure you read the label.

Once selected, take your gemstone-crystals and wash them thoroughly. Remember, these stones have come from all four corners of the earth. To be sure, I sterilise mine by boiling them for at least a minute. Once cleaned, then you can dedicate your crystal by saying something like:

"I dedicate this crystal to love and will only use it for the Universal benefit for all."

In esoteric terms, this forms part of a spiritual ritual.

Then place the stones-crystals into the first bottle full of water, and screw the top back on. Now place a label on this bottle (sticky address labels are ideal) just saying 'Elixir'. Now place the bottle onto a window sill for three days and three nights, following the way Hildegard seems to have been instructed.

Note the time, and for the next two days or nights 'visit' the bottle at the same time, and touch it. While you do so, imagine your desired effects, but especially imagine how you will feel when they are achieved. Start building up the anticipation.

On the third day or night take the bottle from the window and shake it, to add energy, and pour the water into the other bottle. You now have your Elixir. Take the stones, dry them and place them into a safe place ready for the next time. Some people like to put them into a silk purse, whilst others will plant them in the earth to re-energise. Others again lay the stones onto much larger pieces of rock crystal or amethyst. Do which ever feels comfortable for you. There are no hard and fast rules that I've ever come across. It's whatever feels right to you.

How to use

We now have the elixir, and the best way I know of using it is as follows. Take the bottle to bed with you, and just before you are about to go to sleep, take a small sip whilst at the same time using a visualisation to imagine the effect you desire to bring about. Add feeling and emotion to your thoughts by believing it's already happened. In other words, how will you feel when you do achieve your goals, your desires?

Therefore I tell you, whatever you ask for in prayer,
Believe that you have received it,
And it will be yours.

Mark 11-24.

Repeat these steps again first thing in the morning - and I do mean first thing, the very first thing, before even getting out of bed. You are trying to catch yourself still in the alpha state of mind. Once you can do this automatically, without thinking, you will have reached the level of mind where these things seem to work.

Place the bottle back in the fridge for storage during the day and bring it out again just before bedtime. Do this for seven consecutive days and nights, and Universal Life Force can't fail to get your message.

And finally ...

In hypnosis, if you give a person a glass of water and instruct them to "take a sip", then tell them they have just taken a truth serum and ask them a question, they will be compelled to tell you the truth, irrespective of the consequences. Be in no doubt.

Imagine telling a person so shy that they have drunk a new drug that's just come onto the market and causes everyone who takes it to just ooze an amazing confidence, becoming so attractive to the opposite sex that they attract admirers like a magnet. There's no doubt that this person will. Or you could tell them they are so confident that they can't possibly fail their exams, or their driving test ...

The processes governing our subconscious mind, the power behind our imagination, our physical and emotional well-being, are all deeply rooted and nourished from the source of Life itself. The ability to contact this deeper source of life comes from within. So enjoy your journey of discovery. It's your journey.

Illustration by ***Rachel Lubinski***

Although the following information is not authoritative,
it is a fluid interpretation from many sources.

Any information given in this book is not intended to be taken
as a replacement for medical advice.
Any person with a condition requiring medical attention should
consult a qualified doctor or therapist.
On no account should a gemstone or crystal ever be swallowed.

RED JASPER A powerful healing stone, can help those suffering from emotional problems. Its power to give strength and console such sufferers is well known. Good for: kidneys, bladder; improves the sense of smell.

ROSE QUARTZ Healing qualities for the mind. Gives help with migraine and headaches. Good for: spleen, kidneys and circulatory system. Coupled with Hematite, works wonders on aches and pains throughout the body.

BLACK ONYX It can give a sense of courage and helps to discover truth. Instils calm & serenity. Good for: bone marrow, relief of stress.

MOTHER OF PEARL Aptly dubbed the sea of tranquillity. Calms the nerves. Good for: calcified joints, digestive system.

TIGER EYE Inspires brave but sensible behaviour. The confidence stone. Good for: liver, kidneys, bladder. Invigorates and energises.

CARNELIAN A very highly-evolved healer. Good for: rheumatism, depression, neuralgia. Helps regularise the menstrual cycle.

GREEN AVENTURINE Stabilises through inspiring independence. Acts as a general tonic. Good for: skin conditions, losing anxiety and fears.

RHODONITE Improves the memory, reduces stress. Good for: emotional trauma, mental breakdown, spleen, kidneys, heart and blood.

SODALITE Imparts youth and freshness. Calms and clears the mind. When combined with Rhodonite, can produce the Elixir of Life.

OBSIDIAN SNOWFLAKE A powerful healer. Brings insight and understanding, wisdom and love. Good for: eyesight, stomach and intestines.

BLUE AGATE Improves the ego. A stone of strength and courage; a supercharger of energy. Good for: stress, certain ear disorders.

AMETHYST Aids creative thinking. Relieves insomnia when placed under pillow. Good for: blood pressure, fits, grief and insomnia.

HEMATITE A very optimistic inspirer of courage and magnetism. Lifts gloominess. Good for: blood, spleen; generally strengthens the body.

ROCK CRYSTAL Enlarges the aura of everything near to it and acts as a catalyst to increase the healing powers of other minerals. Good for: brain, soul; dispels negativity in your own energy field.

MOONSTONE Gives inspiration and enhances the emotions. A good emotional balancer and solid friend, inspiring wisdom. Good for: period pain and kindred disorders, fertility and child-bearing.

o0o

You can use any of the gemstones or crystals mentioned here for your elixir. The following lists have all been taken from my various books; they may help you to decide. Also, to help, here are a few suggestions for that special elixir:

LOVE .... Rose Quartz, Amethyst & Carnelian

PEACE.............. Green Aventurine, Rose Quartz & Rhodonite

GOOD LUCK ..... Moonstone, Green Aventurine & Obsidian Snowflake

FERTILITY......... Rock Crystal, Rose Quartz & Moonstone

ENERGY............ Amethyst, Rock Crystal & Carnelian

HEALING .... Rock Crystal, Red Jasper & Carnelian

CONFIDENCE... Tiger Eye, Green Aventurine & Black Onyx

PROSPERITY.... Green Aventurine & Obsidian Snowflake

ELIXIR of LIFE... Rhodonite & Sodalite

FRIENDSHIP ..... Moonstone, Carnelian & Amethyst

See your local stockist for any Gemstones and Crystals mentioned in this publication.

However, if you are having difficulty in obtaining any of the stones mentioned, we do offer our own mail order service and would be more than pleased to supply any of the stones listed.

Most Gemstones and Crystals, with just a few exceptions - for example Mother of Pearl - can be supplied in the form of Tumblestones. These are smooth, rounded stones ideal for use as a Birthstone or as Healing Crystals. The nature of Mother of Pearl, and one or two others, prevents them being supplied as Tumblestones; however, we would be pleased to supply these in their natural form.

For further details - write to:

ROSEWOOD
P.O. Box 219, Huddersfield, West Yorkshire. HD2 2YT

E-mail enquiries to: info@rosewood-gifts.co.uk

Or why not visit our website for even more information:

www.rosewood-gifts.co.uk

*Other titles in the **'POWER FOR LIFE'** series:*

Discover your own Special Birthstone and the renowned Healing Powers of Crystals REF. (BK1) A look at Birthstones, personality traits and characteristics associated with each Sign of the Zodiac – plus a guide to the author's own unique range of Power Gems.

A Special Glossary of Healing Stones plus Birthstones REF. (BK2) An introduction to Crystal Healing, with an invaluable Glossary listing common ailments and suggesting combinations of Gemstones/Crystals.

Create a Wish Kit using a Candle, a Crystal and the Imagination of Your Mind REF. (BK3) 'The key to happiness is having dreams; the key to success is making dreams come true.' This book will help you achieve.

Crystal Pendulum for Dowsing REF. (BK5) An ancient knowledge for unlocking your Psychic Power, to seek out information not easily available by any other means. Contains easy-to-follow instructions.

Crystal Healing – Fact or Fiction? Real or Imaginary? REF. (BK6) Find the answer in this book. Discover a hidden code used by Jesus Christ for healing, and read about the science of light and colour. It's really amazing.

How to Activate the Hidden Power in Gemstones and Crystals REF. (BK7) The key is to energise the thought using a crystal. The conscious can direct – but discover the real power. It's all in this book.

Astrology: The Secret Code REF. (BK8) In church it's called 'Myers Briggs typology'. In this book it's called 'psychological profiling'. If you read your horoscope, you need to read this to find your true birthstone.

Talismans, Charms and Amulets REF. (BK9) Making possible the powerful transformations which we would not normally feel empowered to do without a little extra help. Learn how to make a lucky talisman.

A Guide to the Mysteries surrounding Gemstones & Crystals REF. (BK10) Crystal healing, birthstones, crystal gazing, lucky talismans, elixirs, crystal dowsing, astrology, rune stones, amulets and rituals.

A Simple Guide to Gemstone & Crystal Power – a mystical A-Z of stones REF. (BK11) From Agate to Zircon, all you ever needed or wanted to know about the mystical powers of gemstones and crystals.

Change Your Life by Using the Most Powerful Crystal on Earth REF. (BK12) The most powerful crystal on earth can be yours. A book so disarmingly simple to understand, yet with a tremendous depth of knowledge.

All the above books are available from your local stockist,
or, if not, from the publisher.

NOTES

Welcome to the world of Rosewood

An extract from a 'thank- you' letter for one of my books.

"I realised just how much you really had indeed understood me and my need for direction and truly have allowed me the confidence and strength to know and believe I can achieve whatever I want in life"